Words of Inspiration
from My
ANGEL

Words of
Inspiration
from My
ANGEL

Dear Maureen & Dave,

Best wishes.
Enjoy reading my lines

Love Mary xx

MARIE DOREATHY

Paperback: 978-1-63767-250-1
eBook: 978-1-63767-251-8

Ordering Information:

BookTrail Agency
8838 Sleepy Hollow Rd.
Kansas City, MO 64114

Printed in the United States of America

CONTENTS

ALL ALONE

He lived alone, he did not care,
he did not want anyone there.
His family he did not want to see,
and lived his life alone in misery.

ALONE EVERY DAY
OF THE YEAR

Sitting lonely on their own
no one to visit, all alone.
No one to talk to,
no one to say,
would you like a glass of sherry
on this Christmas day.

Where are the families that they once knew,
sitting alone feeling so blue.
Mum, Dad you will be alright,
we will come and visit one of these nights.

To have a bit of company once more,
to hear a knock at their door.
The days are short, the nights so long.
These old folks just carry on.

A Message from an Angel

Have you ever found a white feather,
in a place it should not have been,
well how on earth did it get there,
from an Angel that cannot be seen.

They say that they walk beside us,
and this I believe to be true,
for today I found a white feather
from an angel that looks after you.

Am I a Paredolia?

Faces in the carpets,
faces on the wall,
faces on the bedclothes,
faces in the hall.

Faces all around me,
faces do I see,
some that are distorted,
looking back at me.

Faces in the clouds,
as they pass on by,
slowly disappearing in the bright sky,
faces in the shadows
looking back at me,
faces in reflections
some perfect as can be.

Faces that have deformity,
startling as can be,
faces all around me,
looking back at me.

Why do I see these faces
everywhere I look?
Is it my imagination,
it says so in the book.

As THE SUN FINALLY SETS

When the sun goes down,
and has finally set for me,
do not cry for me,
just set me free.

As I journey to my heavenly home,
remember I am no longer alone.
This is a journey we all must take,
do not cry for me for goodness sake.

I will be watching over you,
guiding you whatever you do.
Just set me free,
Just let me go,
for I have always loved you so.

Remember the good times I spent with you,
the laughter, the tears I shared with you.
Do not cry for me on this day,
for I won't be too far away.

Set me free, just let me go,
do not cry for me,
for I shall know.

THE BLUEBELL WOOD

Today I walked in the bluebell wood,
what a beautiful sight to see,
to stroll amongst the bluebells,
in peace and tranquillity.

The sun was shining brightly,
the day was warm and dry,
there in the bluebell wood,
I sat down and cried.

Remembering my days with you,
you're now a long time gone,
down in the bluebell wood,
humming your favourite song.

Down in the bluebell wood,
alone I sat and cried,
down in the bluebell wood,
I buried you when your died.

When my time has finally come,
you may lay me here to rest,
down in the bluebell wood,
this place I love the best.

CHRISTMAS

Partridge, Pheasant, Turkey or Duck,
hanging in the butchers shop.
decorations on the wall,
Christmas tree in the hall.

A kiss beneath the mistletoe,
open fires all aglow,
presents beneath the decorated tree,
I wonder what they could be.

Carols in the village square,
this beautiful music through the air.
you're soft hand held in mine,
a glass or two of warm mulled wine.

Gentle rides on a sleigh,
snowball fights and laughter share,
Toys in the curiosity shop,
made the children look and stop.

Christmas from long ago,
So romantic we will never know.

CHRISTMAS PRESENTS

He gave me a beautiful nightie,
and said I look good in bed,
he wanted me to look sexy
with a scarf on my head.

Also a cuddly teddy,
and hankies for my nose,
a beautiful bunch of roses,
and socks for my toes.

A beautiful ring that sparkles bright
he gave to me on Christmas night.
lots and lots of chocolates,
for these I do not share.
He said I was his sweetie
he told me how much he cared.

He asked me to get married,
I should be his wife
Oh what a beautiful present.
on this Christmas night.

CONTROL OVER HER LIFE

I am going to tell you how it's going to be,
you are going to spend your life with me,
I am in control, day and night,
I dont want to get in a fight.

With all my money from the dole,
down to the betting shop I will stroll.
Give me your money in your bag,
I am going to bet it on a nag.

I hit you and you are brave,
just remember you are my slave,
I want my food, I want it now,
off to the kitchen you lazy cow.

I don't care what people think,
some people say I need a shrink,
you may say that I am mad,
my answer to you,
you are sad.

I will always rule your life,
remember I am your husband,
you are my wife.
In this home I am the boss,
and you know I dont give a toss.
So dont forget I'm watching you.
you just do as I tell you.

DNA THE TRUTH

What is your reasoning,
why can't you see,
open your minds to reality,
why on earth, don't you want to know,
there is no denying it tells us so.
DNA testing don't tell a lie,
DNA testing, we cannot deny.

Why did you accuse me of causing such pain?
tell me the reasons, what can you gain,
open your minds to reality,
DNA testing you know it is me.

A blood relation I came from the past,
abandoned at birth, now found at last,
what is your reasoning, why can't you see?
DNA testing-Yes this is me.

FLOWERS OF THE MONTH

Flowers for my grave.

January: Snowdrops
If I should die in January,
lay snowdrops on my grave.

February: Primroses.
If it should be February
when skies are dark and bleak,
leave some lovely primroses,
each day of the week.

March: Daffodils
March should be more pleasant,
with daffodils in bloom,
it tells us spring is on its way,
no more doom and gloom.

April: Sweet Peas
Now April comes, and sweet peas grow,
a beautiful flower for all to show,
standing tall in splendour and serene,
a flower not so often seen.

May: Lily of the Valley & Chrysanthemum
If I should die in the month of May,
some lovely flowers will do,
but please don't leave Chrysanthemum
or I will haunt you.

June: Honeysuckle & Roses
Yellow roses are my favourite,
Red or Pink won't do,
I insist they must be yellow,
to stop you feeling blue.

July: Lily and Larkspur
These flowers I do not know,
but at the end my darling,
I will leave it up to you.

August: Poppies and Gladiolus
Again, such beautiful flowers,
poppies so wild and true,
reminds me of the soldiers,
who died to free me and you.

September: Aster & Morning Glory
I don't know much about these flowers,
I wonder if you do?

October: Marigolds
These flowers with their strong smell,
please don't leave for I can tell.

November: Chrysanthemum
These flowers I dislike.

December: Holly
The Holly with its berries so red,
another one of my favourites,
even when I am dead.
There are lots of flowers that I like,
and plenty of choice for you,
please do forgive me.
If I only mentioned a few.

FOR SOMEONE SPECIAL IN MY LIFE

If only you were happy,
and spend more time alone,
if only you were free today,
and had more time to roam.

If only we could say the words,
that wouldn't make you cry.
As you travel on your lonely road,
you know we will be there
to comfort you at the waiting end,
for you know that we care.

Life is what you make it,
and you have made your vow.
Now vows they can be broken,
maybe not today,
sometime in the future
your sorrow will go away.

GONE FOREVER

You up and left me on this day,
Many words I still had to say,
You committed suicide,
What could we do?

We had lived together for so long,
until another woman came along.
She took my love from you,
nothing more could I say or do.

You pleaded with me to stay,
and not leave on this day.

Many years have now passed by,
I question myself "Why did you die"
Alone I sit and sometimes cry.
I missed you for a long time,
but life goes on and all is fine.
No-one wins to this day,
nothing more left to say.

If I could call you in heaven,
and tell you how much I cared,
I am only left with your memories
for these I cannot share.

HEAVEN AND HELL

They say that there is Heaven,
they also say there is Hell
Is this where all the bad souls go,
how on earth can they tell?

If there is a Heaven,
the bible tells us so,
is this the Heaven
where our souls go.

HOARDERS

Why in our life do we need more stuff,
in this life do we not have enough?
It is only clutter at the end of the day,
no longer needed when we fade away.

The families they all come around,
to see whatever they can scrounge,
they could not be bothered in their life
to visit relatives when they were alive.

They crawl from out of the woodwork to see,
which items that may be going free,
I'll have this you can hear them say,
Oh I saw it first, that is mine,
these words you hear every time.

I WONDER WHY?

Did you ever stop and wonder why?
he looks so sad, his skin so dry,
his hair is also very long,
what on earth could have gone wrong.

Was he handsome in his youth?
did he have a family?
only he knows the truth.
How many roads will he walk each day?
In all sorts of weather, when skies are grey.

Sleeping on a cardboard box,
on the streets totally lost.
Nowhere now he can call his home,
trudging the streets, he now roams.
I Wonder Why?

Many people say, "It is his choice",
how do we know we only surmise?
we ask no questions, we pass him by,
why should we comment.
I Wonder Why.
No one stops, they pass him by,
this lonely man,
I Wonder Why.

IS IT A DREAM?

Angels floating everywhere,
soft sweet music fills the air.
floating on a mystic cloud.
No words spoken from their mouths.

Smiles upon their soft face
peace at last I embrace,
soft white clouds like cotton wool,
faces appearing in every one
Am I dreaming,was I there.

IN MY DREAM WITH YOU

Last night I had a lovely dream,
in this dream I was with you,
you kissed me gently on my lips
I returned my kisses to you.

This dream was all distorted,
but did not last too long,
your wife was in another room
you said our love was strong.

I awoke to find,
It was only just a dream,
I never met this man before
but oh was he so real.

LIFE IS NO DRESS REHEARSAL

You made me laugh, you made me cry,
you felt my sadness and understood why.
Feeling so all alone,
struggling to cope on my own.
Life is for living,
don't waste time with eternal grieving.

MENTAL ILLNESS

She would not admit to being unwell,
and gave me many years of hell.
Accusations were many,
accused of Murder, Robbery as well
I knew this woman was not well.

Accused of selling drugs by the dozen
Incestous affairs with my brother,
Running a brothel just for men,
I wouldn't know where to begin.

This woman is not well,
and refuses to take a pill.
Did I really steal her money,
I did not find this very funny.

I began to question myself
"Was I losing the plot"
Pull yourself together,-I was not.
If mental illness knocks on your door
have compassion for this person for sure.
There is nothing that you can do
They will blame it all on you,

MISSING YOU

I miss you day and night,
the days roll on, the nights too long.
I wish that you were here right now,
you left me for some old cow.

Come back to me in a while,
I shed each tear with a smile,
It's been a very long time.
Although you are gone,
my love for you lingers on
my heart weeps without you,
alone I am missing you.

MY FRIEND

Caught a glimpse of my friend today,
Inverse of life she had much to say,
of love requited and unrequited,
of death but after life united.
Of relationships both good and bad,
of bodily functions we've all had.
Valentines and Christmas day,
the way life flows in many ways.
But most of all that we should drive
to be kind, be happy and glad to be alive.

No Peace

They will wear you down,
they will not give in,
they will wear you down,
it's such a sin.

They will wear you down,
until they are through,
they will wear you down,
and are trained to do.

They cannot see that you are right,
they are blinkered through day and night,
They will wear you down,
they will not give in,
Well why should you.

Who on earth do they think they are
no compassion, they have no heart,
They will make sure they do their best
you get no peace, you get no rest.

To them, it doesn't matter if you are feeling blue,
they will wear you down,--
for that is what they do.

OUR OLD AGE PENSIONER HOLIDAY

She was an elderly lady
well in her later years,
Can you take me on holiday,
for this I did fear.

We headed on our holiday,
to a holiday camp unknown
she said it was a lovely place,
and sure I would not moan.

I asked along a couple of friends,
not wanting to be on my own
with this dear old pensioner,
who did not want to be alone

We arrived at our destination
a holiday by the sea,
full of all the old folks,
with their mobility,
scooter galore,
lots and lots of Zimmer frames,
which they left by their doors.

The camp was really scruffy,
the carpets were ragged and torn
we might as well enjoy ourselves
no point in having a moan.

All meals were at a set time,
do not be late or you won't dine
the staff were really shirty,
The food was really yucky
we won't go there any more.

The old folks who we met each day,
we gave them all a good laugh,
with our tales from our past
were happy and bright we say.

The swimming pool was out of action,
waters so green, no satisfaction.
we headed down to the shore,
to wet our feet and more.

Our week came to an end,
the old pensioner enjoyed herself,
I am so sorry to say,
she is not with us today.

OLD AGE REGRETS

Married for a long long time,
all alone now and feeling blue,
he now wondered what he should do.

She cooked, she washed, she looked after him well,
now all alone no one he tells,
of all thing things she used to do,
to make him comfortable his whole life through.

He took her for granted, she was his wife,
her duty was to help him survive,
his money he did not spend,
watching his pennies wherever he went.

Now that he is old and grey,
his money won't give away,
He misses her now that she has gone,
and asks himself where he went wrong.

You cannot look back on your life,
wishing for things that you despised,
Her life could have been kinder,
I hear him say,
if she was still with me today.

R.I.P

As they laid you to rest,
we all stood and cried,
you were loved by all you knew,
at home and far awide.

God took you too early,
in life you were not well,
you were not meant to suffer,
to live a life of hell.

SLOGGIES

I love to wear my sloggies,
they hide a lot of flesh,
I love to wear my sloggies,
they come up to my chest.

Unlike the sexy G-Strings
that go up your crack,
my sloggies are real comfortable,
they hide my rolls of flab.

You may think I am old fashioned,
you are all wrong you see,
I wear the latest fashions,
G-strings not for me.

SOME FAMILIES DO NOT CARE

They stood and cried,
as they laid her to rest,
Oh yes dear Mum,
you were one of the best.

Do not worry Mum, things will be fine
we will visit when we have time.
for days on end she spent at home.
Lonely and sad on her own.

Now that she is no longer here,
the sadness, the regrets,
and their tears.
Look after your Mum
I hear them say.
For she will not be with you one day
Goodbye dear Mum you are at rest.

SOMETIMES LIFE IS A STRUGGLE

When things go wrong as they often will,
when the road you travel is a struggle up hill,
when your bank account is very low,
and money is short, where can you go.
No one there to help you out,
you cry, your sad, no way out.
Don't give up, life can be cruel,
your moral is low, you are no fool.
As one door closes, you will succeed,
life seems bad at times indeed.
A silver lining is on the way,
stay positive as you face a new day. ☺

TAKEN BY THE SEA

Where have you gone,
where can you be,
your body was taken by the sea,
they say you drowned,
or were you pushed
we will never know,
you were loved so much.

You were young
and a little wild
was someone jealous,
was someone blind
your body was taken by the sea,
there were no goodbye's
just our hearts full of tears.

THE FAMILY THIEF

He wrote to him a letter.,
to kindly say,
where is my money you borrowed that day.
This old man was so naive,
and by this thief he was deceived.

I'll pay you back so much a month.
Mr thief you are a runt.
A blinking blabber is what I say.
He robbed this old man in every way.

This old man was oh so frail,
and should have taken the thief to jail.
Now this old boy is dead and gone,
but you Mr thief you live on.

THE GARDEN THAT DIED

We had a beautiful garden,
that was always full of bloom,
but since my baby left it,
It has gone to rack and ruin.

The lovely blossom on the trees,
the Jasmin bush beneath the breeze,
they are all now dead and gone,
our beautiful garden what went wrong.

No tender hands to keep it,
no words that I can tell,
the beauty of this garden,
has now gone to hell.

The Cock Inn where we used to sit,
and have a drink or two,
enjoying a glass of sherry,
or maybe a Pimm's would do.

The shelves have all been emptied,
the bar it is no more,
the only things that will remain,
are memories that's for sure.

We can never ever retrieve it,
for its long now dead and gone,
the beauty of this garden,
no longer lingers on.

The Ghost of Marlow Manor

He sat each day on his bench.
life for him was a wrench,
not much left in his life,
no fancy woman, or no wife.

His neighbours they didn't care
too miserable to them
whilst he was there.
his Manor went to rack and ruin,
he spent each day in one room.

Too mean to spend a penny or two
to keep him warm the winter through.
A blanket around him he was too weak,
his future looked rather bleak.

For it was soon meant to be
he passed away miserly
what good did his money do,
a penny he would not give to you.

Now the old bugger is gone,
his ghostly figure still lives on.
he sits outside for some to see,
this is the gospel truth, take it from me.

THE LONG LONELY ROAD

Alone with her memories
from when she was young
wondering in her life,
what she had done.

Travelling back to her birth home,
feeling sad and all alone.
Why did she leave?
She had no choice,
to marry a man
whom she despised.

A prearranged marriage by her Mum and Dad,
A life of unhappiness
not happy but sad.

THE NAUGHTY SIXTIES

One night whilst out on a date,
this young man did not hesitate
to show me his willie,
he acted so silly,
one night whilst out on a date.

He came from over the hill,
and said his dolly was ill,
could I give it a stroke,
he was having a joke,
this young man from over the hill.

THE NIT NURSE

When I was young and very bold,
my hair was long and golden.
The little buggers they got to me,
for all the classroom to see.

I scratched my head, day and night
and made it bleed Oh what a sight.

My dad took me to the nurse,
to rid me of these little turs,
she cut my hair way too short,
made me look like a boy,
my school friends laughed
and made me cry.

I hated school from that day on,
lots of days on the run,
some day I just refused to go,
played truant, my parents did not know.

My education was somewhat weak,
My teachers said my future looked bleak.

THE PAEDOPHILE

What could I do,
for I was young,
this paedophile was my old man.

I did not know this was wrong,
of the things he used to do,
for his was my old man.

An innocent child in every way,
he kissed my ear,
as he did say,
please do not tell your mum,
he knew he was doing wrong.

It was into my teenage years,
when the abusing did stop,
I kept it locked in my mind,
one day he lost the plot.

He one day got annoyed,
and beat me black and blue,
kicked me violently in my ribs,
and broke quite a few.

It was the jealousy of this man,
himself a victim of abuse,
no longer could he abuse me,
for him there was no excuse.

Older and much wiser,
I look back on my life
I do not hate my old man
it was he who gave me life.

The Robin for Natalie and Teresa

In Peter's memory

A little robin flew in today,
he sat on the rafters as if to say,
I was wondering if you are all fine,
I know it was around this time.

I left you and said goodbye,
many tears were shed you all did cry.
My spirit is with you today,
I came as a robin to watch over you,
I am proud of you and all that you do.
remember I will always be with you.

THE VIRUS

From over the mountains and over the sea,
this virus is one we cannot see.
It has taken the lives of thousands or more,
the future ahead there will be more.

Some people are idiots, they think they know best,
they venture out putting people at risk.
Why do they not listen?
Why can't they see.
they could end up in the Mortuary.

It don't matter if you are rich or poor,
it could come knocking at your door,
listen to the government, they know best,
everybody is at risk.

Don't venture out,
please stay well,
hopefully this virus,
will end up in hell.

VISITING ANNE BRONTE RESTING PLACE

As she lay beneath the earth,
her words they came into my head.
Words she penned from long ago,
tales to tell of Ill and woe.

TRUE LOVE

The sweet smell of roses you gave to me,
your loving kisses that were meant to be,
you had me at your fingertips,
as you kissed my tender lips.

For every kiss you gave to me,
with all my heart I could see,
no more should we part,
forever you will stay in my heart.

Now that I am old and grey,
these feelings just won't go away,
I often long for your soft touch,
and would love to love you oh so much.

Our love between us is so true,
I still love you, yes, I do,
but age is not on our side,
only God will decide.

TRY NOT TO FORGET

Looking through the window of my mind,
the shadows of memories I leave behind,
where have they gone I do not know,
that was not so long ago.

Memories are weak as I go on,
memories don't stay around too long,
my memory fades as times unfolds,
my memories fades as I grow old.

My memory forgets for a while,
were you here in time,
like the shadows that fade in the dark,
forgetting things, we did in the past,
were you really here.

I look at your photo it jogs my mind,
memorising times when you were so kind,
days, months and years pass by,
my memory is fading it's saying goodbye.
I try not to forget the past,
my memory is fading it won't last.

YOU CAME TO MIND TODAY

As I look at our photos I recall,
the laughter, the tears, the years
we shared now gone,
only memories are left behind,
you are no longer here.
Life seems so unfair,
we cannot even share
the memories when we were young,
now a long time gone.

If only we could see ahead,
given a choice, maybe once, or maybe twice,
would life be different in any way,
for the future we cannot see.
Don't wish for things,
don't wish for what life may bring,
be content with what you've got,
for memories they can mean a lot.

WHENEVER I VISIT MY MUM'S GRAVE

I leave a flower for the lady buried next to Mum. I have never seen a flower on her grave.

I leave a flower for you.

No flowers by your headstone,
no one to visit you,
did you have a family?
did they once love you?

I visit my mum's place of rest,
a flower I leave for you
although I never knew you,
it is the right thing for me to do.

Is your family long time gone?
or were you all alone,
did you have no-one,
to visit you at home.

No flowers on your headstone,
no one to visit you,
whenever I visit my mum's place of rest
I'll leave a flower for you.

WE ALL LOVE A PUSSY CAT

My friends they had an old cat,
and loved him in every way,
they even took him on holiday,
well what would people say.

I'm sure he looked forward to his holiday,
for this i think he knew,
from Lands end to John o'Groats,
everywhere he did go.

My friends woke up one day
to find him unwell,
he had a stroke the night before,
for this they could tell.

They took him to the PDSA,
the vet said "you must let go",
He put their pussy peacefully to sleep
and now he is no more.

Now if you own a pussy cat,
treat it really well
they know you are their master,
for the pussy cats can tell.

WHERE DO OUR SOULS GO?

Where do our souls go when we die?
Are we a star in the clear night sky?
maybe a flower that blooms in spring,
 do we become anything.
A cloud that passes slowly by,
a teardrop that falls when we cry.

A sun beam on a bright summer day,
a breeze of wind that passes our way,
a butterfly with beautiful wings,
could we be any one of these things?

Angel we cannot see,
 beautiful mermaid from the sea,
a bird that flies oh so high.
Where do our souls go when we die?
we will never know, I wonder why.

WHERE ARE YOU NOW

Sleepless nights thinking of you,
tossing and turning Oh what can I do,
where are you now, where have you gone,
Sleepless nights Oh what have I done.

Many a night we sat and talked,
what good did it do, you still walked,
where are you now, where can you be,
you left me alone in misery.

Tell me you care, I want to hear,
I'm all alone now, crying my tears,
what can I do, what do you care?
tossing and turning that's not fair.

Please let me know if you are well,
just tell me you care for I can tell,
maybe in time you will come to me,
maybe in time you will see,
what you have missed, it's only fair,
sleepless nights what do you care.

Tell me you want me,
I hope it is true,
Tossing and turning thinking of you.

WHERE DO YOU BELONG?

Born for adoption and given away,
no love from your mother,
nothing to say.
How can we find you,
where can you be,
Are you a neighbour,
Do you know me?

Rejected by your mother,
with a heart cold as ice,
deceiving her family,
with her life full of lies.

Was it a denial you no longer exist,
where are the years,
they have now missed.
She kept it a secret,
like a dark cloud,
a son and a daughter,
she should have been proud.

WOODLAND BURIAL

To the beautiful woodland burial,
I want to go when I die,
To the woodland place where I shall rest,
This woodland burial would be the best.

Take me god it is not too late,
take me now don't make me wait.
I cannot live another day,
please dont let me die in this way.

Please let me jump the queue,
So now that I can be with you.
You will just have to wait,
when it is your turn,
God will not hesitate.
Please don't leave me in this pain,
take me now God to your heavenly plane.